Contents

TO LEARN MORE about Unitarian Universalism or to locate a congregation near you, please visit the Unitarian Universalist Association at uua.org. We welcome you to join us for faith development and worship, where we strive to connect with one another with respect, openness, and understanding. You can also follow the Unitarian Universalist Association on Facebook and Bluesky.

Unitarian Universalist Association
24 Farnsworth Street
Boston, MA 02210-1409
(617) 742-2100
uua.org

THE LARGEST UU CONGREGATION is the Church of the Larger Fellowship, a congregation with no geographical boundary. The CLF creates global spiritual community, rooted in profound love, which cultivates wonder, imagination, and the courage to act. Members live all over the world and interact with the fully remote church staff by mail, phone, email, and social media.

Church of the Larger Fellowship
24 Farnsworth Street
Boston, MA 02210-1409
(617) 948-6166
clfuu.org

Shared Unitarian Universalist Values and Inspirations

As Unitarian Universalists, we covenant, congregation to congregation and throughout our Unitarian Universalist Association, to support and assist one another in our ministries. We draw from our heritages of freedom, reason, hope, and courage, building on the foundation of love.

Love is the power that holds us together and is at the center of our shared values. We are accountable to one another for doing the work of living our shared values through the spiritual discipline of love.

Inseparable from one another, these shared values are:

Interdependence. We honor the interdependent web of all existence. With reverence for the great web of life and with humility, we acknowledge our place in it.

We covenant to protect the Earth and all beings from exploitation. We will create and nurture sustainable relationships of care, respect, mutuality, and justice. We will work to repair harms and damaged relationships.

Pluralism. We celebrate that we are all sacred beings, diverse in culture, experience, and theology.

We covenant to learn from one another in our free and responsible search for truth and meaning. We embrace our differences and commonalities with love, curiosity, and respect.

Justice. We work to be diverse, multicultural, beloved communities where all thrive.

We covenant to dismantle racism and all forms of systemic oppression. We support the use of inclusive democratic processes to make decisions within our congregations, our Unitarian Universalist Association, and society at large.

Transformation. We adapt to the changing world.

We covenant to collectively transform and grow spiritually and ethically. Openness to change is fundamental to our Unitarian and Universalist heritages, never complete and never perfect.

Generosity. We cultivate a spirit of gratitude and hope.

We covenant to freely and compassionately share our faith, presence, and resources. Our generosity connects us to one another in relationships of interdependence and mutuality.

Equity. We declare that every person is inherently worthy and has the right to flourish with dignity, love, and compassion.

We covenant to use our time, wisdom, attention, and money to build and sustain fully accessible and inclusive communities.

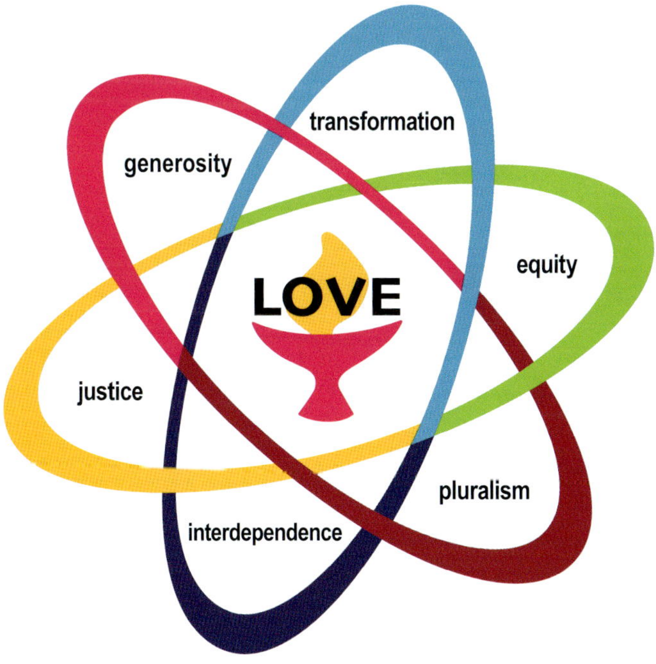

Inspirations

Direct experiences of transcendent mystery and wonder are primary sources of Unitarian Universalist inspiration. These experiences open our hearts, renew our spirits, and transform our lives. We draw upon and are inspired by sacred, secular, and scientific understandings that help us make meaning and live into our values. These sources ground us and sustain us in ordinary, difficult, and joyous times. We respect the histories, contexts, and cultures in which these sources were created and are currently practiced. Grateful for the experiences that move us, aware of the religious ancestries we inherit, and enlivened by the diversity that enriches our faith, we are called to ever deepen and expand our wisdom.

Preface

Rev. Dr. Sofía Betancourt

Beloved, you are welcome here.

Whether you are just learning about Unitarian Universalism, are deepening your connection to a UU community, or are a longtime member of this living tradition wanting to engage with its central values and commitments, I hope the offerings in this book will be helpful to you. We are a place of particular welcome for the curious. The drive to ask questions and engage lovingly with others who are about the task of meaning making is part of what makes Unitarian Universalism such a valuable communal space to many.

As you will learn in the pages that follow, Unitarian Universalism is a religion full of seeming contradictions that, in fact, animate the practice of our faith. Unlike many organized religions, we do not lay claim to one clearly delineated theological truth, yet we do have a deep and powerful theology. We do not offer answers, but instead companion each other in exploring life's deepest questions. Ours is not a community of shared belief, but a community of shared values with a commitment to practicing those values in ways that create a better world. There is no test for belonging here. We are bound together by a covenant of how we will be with one another and the shared values we will promote in the world. We elevate the use of reason and the freedom of belief. Ours is a tradition that is committed to reviewing our shared values periodically, and we did so most recently at our General Assembly in 2024.

The power that holds us together is love. Not an emotional love motivated by affection, but the spiritual discipline of love rooted in the nonnegotiable sacredness of each and every person and, indeed, of all life. Unitarian Universalist congregations and communities create the opportunity for people with vastly different answers to life's big questions—where did consciousness come from, what holds the universe together, what happens after death—to be in real, deep relationship with each other, communally caring for one another, and building solidarity across lines of profound difference.

In this way, we practice building a world where difference does not divide us, where people of different backgrounds, religions, nations, and identities live free from violence, hatred, and dehumanization. "How we relate to each other creates the conditions of hell or heaven here on earth," as Rev. Deanna Vandiver teaches us. "We are all in this together."

With its commitment to welcome, love, grow, and serve, Unitarian Universalism strives to provide a vital alternative to the growing tide of separation, loneliness, exclusion, and control that is rising around the world. As inheritors of religious teachings that have long been counter-cultural, and longer than long insisted on leading with love, we work both to provide sanctuary—spiritual, emotional, and physical—and to counter the forces of intolerance and hate in our wider world.

On the cover of this pocket guide is a stylized flaming chalice, a primary symbol of Unitarian Universalism. It has a history of signifying sanctuary and assistance for those fleeing fascism in Europe under Nazi rule. Today, with fascism on the rise once more, our flaming chalice is a fiery reminder of the commitments of our faith, commitments that invite each and every one of us to risk what we think we know about the power of love in the world for greater freedoms, greater justice, and, ultimately, liberation for all.

Unitarian Universalism places that love at the center of our living tradition. It is a love that sets us free. Not *free* as in having the power to do whatever we want, but *free* as in not weighed down or bound by the patterns of hatred and control that get passed from generation to generation. *Free* as in restless and called to solidarity wherever we witness injustice. *Free* as in knowing without a doubt that we are worthy and that it is ours to invite others into the same wisdom about themselves. Free. Free to imagine a world where children are not in harm's way, where the violence and desperation of generations have served as a site of sacred repair, interrupting the cycles of war and dehumanization. Free. Free to express our highest values and what we believe in as many poetic forms as there are people in the room. Free to build communities that love us enough that we are held when we falter and invited back into sacred covenant when we fail.

And we know it is not enough to simply say that love lives at the center of our tradition. We must also ask what it means to live as if love itself matters. If the task of living guided by inclusive, progressive values in a pluralistic community that honors all life is compelling to you, I hope you will find your place among us to share in this sacred journey together.

For Unitarian Universalists, life on earth can be so vast, so magnificent, so challenging that many perspectives are needed to approach it. On the surface, our perspectives may have little in common. Some of us draw on nature, some on science, some on human experience, and some on spiritual tradition. Still, we are held together—thanks to these varied perspectives—by common values that grow from our plurality. When we "live into" these values, we center love, strive for justice, practice generosity, and more. In all these ways, we seek to be like a vibrant and intricate ecosystem, animated as much by collectivity as uniqueness.

—Rev. Karen Van Fossan

Our Theology

Rev. Dr. Sheri Prud'homme

Whether you are new to Unitarian Universalism or newly curious, welcome! In these next few pages, I hope to orient you to some core aspects of Unitarian Universalist theology. *Theology* is a word not all Unitarian Universalists find comfortable. Some think of theology as belonging only to classical Christianity, which is not congruent with their experience of the religiously pluralistic, scientifically grounded, open, and affirming Unitarian Universalist communities they have come to know. As a Unitarian Universalist theologian and religious educator, I love theology. I use the word more broadly. Theology is about the nature of being human, how we are related to all that exists, how we are related to the ultimate ground of being, and how we understand the horizon toward which all life is oriented. In my view, how we understand and speak of these things matters—in our families, communities, and broader society.

Our understandings shape our beliefs, our actions, and our imagination of what is possible.

To acquaint you with key aspects of our theology, I will build on Rev. Dr. Rebecca Parker's metaphor of a theological house or dwelling place, which she introduced in a series of lectures at the Liberal Religious Educators Association Falls Conference in 2002. As a metaphor, it has some apt resonances. It is our location amid all the other houses of worship in our communities. The dwelling place predates your arrival, but your presence among us may change it. It has been built through centuries and is constantly being redecorated, remodeled, and sometimes reconstructed. There's a common phrase among us that "revelation is not sealed"; in other words, our religion is open to being changed by new insights, knowledge, experiences, and understandings. Our forebears, liberal Christians—both Universalists and Unitarians—incorporated historical biblical criticism, looked beyond the Bible to the natural world and human experience as sources of religious truth, folded in the discoveries of science, and continued to evolve in response to an ever-widening circle of voices and perspectives sharing knowledge and insight about what it means to be human and live sustainably with compassion and justice on our planet. How Unitarian Universalists collectively understand our theology is increasingly shaped by feminist, womanist, queer, disability, postcolonial, and liberationist theories and perspectives of recent decades that many of our clergy and congregants hold in high regard. So, whether you imagine this dwelling place as a house, an apartment, a camper van, or a tent, know that it is not static. It has and will continue to change.

We can use this metaphor to speak about several facets of our theology. Let's start with the roof of our theological dwelling place. The roof represents how we understand what shelters or protects life and its corollary—what puts life at risk. We understand that what we need protection from is the human-created structures and systems that endanger and harm life, such as the capacity of humankind to create hell for one another on this earth, the conditions that create violence, oppression, and exploitation. With roots deep in our Universalist heritage, we understand that what saves or redeems us is not death but creative and active love. The great Universalist Rev. Dr. Hosea Ballou wrote in 1805 that Jesus's death on the cross does not save us; rather, he maintained that such an idea harms the spirit of God and allows people to imitate and justify cruelty. Moreover, we inherit from our Universalist forebears the conviction that whatever happens after death happens equally to all, or what they called "universal salvation." There is no "us" who are saved and "them" who are not. Restoration and redemption are what we create in this life on this planet in the here and now. Salvation, then, is in our hands. Some among us would say that we collaborate with a more-than-human force, which may be named in many ways, such as revolutionary Grace, creative Love, Source, the divine, Spirit of Life, God or Goddess, and some among us would say that we act not as humankind alone but in concert with all life. Either way, the focus of our religious life becomes this world in the here and now, where there is a sacred spark in every living thing.

The walls of our dwelling place, to continue the metaphor, are what holds us together in religious community. For us, it is not ancestry, geography, or belief in a creed that binds us; rather, we create congregations and our denominational body, the Unitarian Universalist Association, through our freely chosen association in the form of the covenants or promises we make with one another. Our embrace of participatory democracy joins a long tradition in religious organizations of protest against patterns that concentrate power in the hands of a few. The use of the democratic process has been and continues to be an important component of how we organize and govern ourselves. Although we unite collectively as the Unitarian Universalist Association, each of our congregations oversees and governs itself, something we call "congregational polity."

This brings us, then, to the floor or foundation of our dwelling place—the connection between humankind and the ultimate or divine. Let's start first with the nature of humankind. The early Unitarian Christians in the United States emerged in the 1800s against a theology of total depravity of the human soul espoused by Calvinist Christianity. Instead, early Unitarians believed humans were born in the image of God. The foremost Unitarian preacher of the time, Rev. William Ellery Channing, spoke about the capacities bestowed on humankind by God as "powers of the soul" that could be nurtured and unfolded throughout the course of a lifetime as one became more fully alive through agency and connection with others and with all life. Following from this basic orientation, Unitarians understood that two central responsibilities of humankind were (1) to dismantle structures and barriers to the full flourishing of life and (2) to encourage and facilitate both secular and religious education. Humanism's rise as a dominant theological perspective in Unitarian Universalism later in the twentieth century built on this core religious understanding of the responsibility and capacity of humankind but without the God part. Unitarian Universalism's relatively high estimation of human nature has been challenged by the pervasive and persistent ways humans continue to harm one another and the planet despite knowing better. This has led us to acknowledge the need for more development in our theology and rituals around lamentation, repentance, forgiveness, and community-wide accountability and healing across generations. In addition, some among us have begun to speak not of humans being born in original sin or original blessing but in original struggle, with the line between good and evil running through each human heart.

The nature of humankind is one aspect of the foundation of our dwelling place; the other is the ultimate ground of being/Source/Spirit/God(ess)/the divine. I use the string of words to denote mystery and multiplicity. Some among us speak of a revolutionary Grace inherent in the universe, or a Spirit of Love, or the Ground of all Being, or the Source of Life, or Goddess, or God. As you might observe, even in this incomplete list, divinity is not fundamental to Unitarian Universalist theology. But for those of us who do hold to the existence of the divine, we name it in many ways. As a common invocation to prayer puts it, "God, known to us by many names and by no name fully known." When we speak of God, we are not speaking of a bearded male being in the heavens pulling strings to control life on earth. Our imagination of God has diversified through the centuries in part because the idea that there is a spark of the divine in every being eventually led to the affirmation of all kinds of people in their beautiful array of genders, cultures, sexual orientations, abilities, and bodies. This, in turn, changed our image of God.

Although Unitarian Universalist conceptions of God are many, none suggests God to be all-powerful or fully in charge. We maintain that freedom in some measure, no matter how small, is fundamental to life. We reject conceptions of God that would excuse humankind from responsibility or legitimize injustice or oppression. We also maintain the essential integrity of science and our religion. From as early as the nineteenth century, Unitarians and Universalists, as well as Transcendentalists, who greatly influenced our religious tradition, have studied the world to understand God, including both spiritual and scientific encounters with the nonhuman natural world. Ours is a religious tradition that, in its contemporary pluralistic expression, has evolved in many aspects away from its early liberal Christian roots. Unitarian Universalist theology has room for God both existing and not existing, and simultaneously, we have some boundaries for understandings of God that belong in our theological dwelling place.

From inside the dwelling place of our theological heritage, we can look out the doors and windows and see the other houses of worship. We recognize and respect other faith traditions with which we share our communities as sacred dwelling places. We work with other communities of faith to bring into being shared values such as pluralism, justice, generosity, and equity in the wider society. Our motivation is not conversion but collaboration. We also protest and resist when other religious communities, civic leaders, and individuals act in ways that cause oppression, suffering, and harm. We know ourselves to be responsible for furthering our values as members of the wider ecosystem of the communities in which our congregations reside—our regions, our nations, and our world.

And what about the horizon toward which all life is oriented? Unitarian Universalist theology has parted ways with the classical Christian notion that a battle between good and evil lies at the end of time, fomenting the destruction of this planet so that it can be replaced by something new. We understand that there is no planet B and that all life is connected and inextricably interwoven in natural processes. We understand ourselves to be part of a long process of evolution, although we have troubled the waters around ideas once held by our forebears, such as inevitably linear progress. Many of us place our hope in the possibility of collective healing and liberation such that we create together what some have called the "kingdom of

God" or the "kin-dom of God" on earth in the tradition of the Social Gospel, and others, inspired by the preaching of Rev. Dr. Martin Luther King, Jr., name "beloved community" as our ultimate goal. Others place our hope in the possibility that we are already in paradise, a place where struggles with evil and injustice exist alongside abundant resources of love, care, wisdom, healing, and responsible uses of power. Either way, the task is to live in right relationship with one another and the earth, not only individually but also collectively, in struggle and in joy, dignifying the sacred spark in all life.

Ours is a sturdy dwelling place that has sheltered hundreds of thousands through the centuries. But it is not without flaws. At times in our history, our theology has been complicit with imperialism, eugenics, placing Protestant Christians with European heritage at the pinnacle of social evolution, and other social movements and perspectives that we now decry and for which we are still wrestling with how to seek accountability, healing, and restoration. At the same time, our dwelling place has fueled movements for abolition, women's suffrage, public education, better treatment of people with mental illness, civil rights, ending redlining, equal marriage rights for all, and reducing carbon emissions, among others. As time passes, perhaps there will be some things you will be part of changing about our theological dwelling place, leaving it more aligned with current understandings of mutual liberation, healing and wholeness, and global sustainability. Welcome, and I hope you'll make yourself at home.

Within Unitarian Universalism, I can be an artist and a scientist at the same time. I can be a believer and a skeptic without any sense of contradiction. I am grateful to be part of a religion that allows for many things to be true at once. Being held in community through deep and active love makes this more than possible—it makes it joyful!

—Rev. Dr. Adam Robersmith

Our Worship

Rev. Katie Romano Griffin

Love is at the center of our values as Unitarian Universalists. Not just any love, but the kind of love that is capable of holding all of the joys and sorrows in our hearts. This kind of love is boundless, reaching beyond personal affections and desires to encompass a universal compassion calling us to care for one another deeply. It is the love that calls us in when we make mistakes, offering the grace needed to come into right relationships with others and ourselves. In a world often marked by division and conflict, this love empowers us to rise up for justice, guiding our actions with compassion and integrity. Although it may not dry our tears, it leads us to the community that will. It does not offer false joy, but it guides us to the well of joy, helping us find solace and strength in the shared experiences of our fellow travelers. This love is infinite, asking questions rather than demanding fealty, and it plants seeds in our hearts that grow into deeper love. This is the kind of love we celebrate and learn about when we worship together.

Worship is an interdisciplinary, collaborative effort. Worship teams build their skills, connect to the community's needs, and strengthen the community's bonds of trust all year round. Our services integrate words, art, poetry, music, movement, ritual, and silence. In the past, Unitarian and Universalist ancestors spent hours, days, or even weeks crafting a single sermon meant to last an hour or more, reflecting the deep thought and care that went into every word. Ministers would then travel from congregation to congregation, sharing the same sermon with different communities, a testament to the interconnectedness of the early Unitarian and Universalist movements. Yet, as stirring as these sermons were, they did not reflect the needs of each particular congregation. Today, although our services are crafted to last just one hour, the preparation involved is no less thoughtful. We aim to create worship that is timely, relevant to attendees, and grounded in love—holding people in community as they journey through life while striving to center love. Religious educators, musicians, ministers, lay leaders, and artists in our congregations often begin planning worship months in advance. Themes are decided, stories chosen, music practiced, and art created with the goal of uplifting the community. Each element is carefully considered to ensure that it resonates with the congregation, providing comfort and challenge, solace and inspiration.

Sometimes, however, worship is planned on short notice, shifting in response to the needs of the community to process an event that has shaken our foundations so that love may guide us forward. These moments often reveal the true depth of our commitment to heart-centered worship as the community comes together to create worship that speaks to the urgency of the moment. Many congregations transformed their Sunday programming overnight after difficult elections; the events of January 6, 2020, at the Capitol; and during times of great rage, such as after the extrajudicial killing of George Floyd. These are times when worship meets the moment, creating space for love to come through in the midst of chaos and pain. In these instances, worship becomes not just a weekly ritual but a lifeline—a space where people can gather to process their emotions, find strength in one another, and recommit to the work of justice and healing. This is heart-centered worship at its most powerful, a force that holds us together even when the world seems to be falling apart.

When I asked Rev. Joe Cherry about Unitarian Universalist worship, he said that he often begins with the question, "How does this work (worship) contribute to the vibrancy of the community?" This question is at the heart of what makes UU worship so unique. It is not just about what happens within the walls of the sanctuary on Sunday morning but also about how that experience ripples out into the broader community, inspiring action, fostering connection, and nurturing the spirit. Rev. Cherry shared that worship is deeply collaborative, and he enjoys working with "teams that take risks." Living is a risky business; shouldn't our worship be the same? Indeed, it is through taking risks that we often find the most profound expressions of love and community. One of the risks that Rev. Cherry has taken in his career is working with worship themes and inviting artists of all ages to create something related to the monthly theme, which is then displayed outside the sanctuary for all to see. This practice not only enriches the worship experience but also invites the congregation into a deeper engagement with the themes, encouraging reflection and creativity beyond the Sunday service. Art is an essential way we express ourselves, giving form to the feelings and thoughts that words alone cannot capture. Love moves us to feel in ways that cannot always be expressed in words, and art becomes a vital conduit for those emotions, connecting us to one another and to something larger than ourselves. This is heart-centered worship.

Sometimes, changes happen during a service in response to the moment. This is where trusting the team and the community is critical. It is not unusual in my congregation to change a hymn, a story, or even the entire structure of the service, sometimes as late as Sunday morning, if a worship team member has an insight that "cracks open our hearts." These moments of spontaneity are not disruptions but rather opportunities for deeper connection, allowing the service to evolve in response to the needs and emotions of the community in real time.

For example, at a recent service in my congregation, after the worship associate shared news of a loss in our community, the music team pivoted on the spot to provide space to hold emotions. The piano softly played the hymn "We Laugh, We Cry" in the background as our music director, Gabe Perbieri, said, "This is the moment when we can think about our lives—what's going well, what's not going well, what is hurting us—while also being able to be in community, to share our pain and our happiness." The congregation remained seated as he invited everyone to sing softly to their own hearts and then rise in body or spirit if they had joy or sorrow that they wanted to be witnessed by the congregation. Tears fell. Hearts opened. This is heart-centered worship—an experience that is not just about following a script but about being fully present with one another, allowing love to guide the way.

Rev. Verdis LeVar Robinson, a minister of music and worship arts, advocates for UU services that reach not only "the part of the heart that yearns for justice and wholeness" but also "the part that reaches for joy, or the completeness of the heart that is centered." This insight speaks to the ongoing challenge of creating worship that touches all aspects of the human experience. Although justice and wholeness are crucial, so, too, are joy and the sense of being centered—of feeling whole and at peace within oneself and within the community. In their work, Rev. Robinson is nourishing a choir called the Jubilee Singers, which moves attendees "toward the centered heart through joy." Music, with its ability to bypass the intellect and speak directly to the soul, plays a critical role in heart-centered worship. It can uplift and inspire, bringing a sense of joy and unity that words alone cannot achieve. Rev. Robinson's main aim for worship attendees is that they "leave the space better than when they arrived, head held high, able to navigate a way through things with joy and inspiration." This is the ultimate goal of heart-centered worship—not only to equip us with the tools to think and explore new ways of being but also to stir something deep within us that takes us emotionally and spiritually toward wholeness.

In UU worship, love is not just a feeling; it is a guiding force that calls us into community, challenges us to grow, and uplifts us in times of need. Through heart-centered worship, we find the strength to face life's challenges, the courage to fight for justice, and the support of a community that holds us through life's many ups and downs. This is the essence of UU worship—a practice that not only sustains us but also calls us to grow, reach beyond ourselves, and become the embodiment of the love we seek in the world.

Worship is the commitment of time and space we covenant with one another—returning in faith as an intentional community. We respect our individual experiences while recognizing that we are stronger together. The worship container is expansive in form and function, allowing congregations to meet the moment at each gathering. Our music interweaves our diversity while being equally eclectic—from traditional hymnody, pop, rap, protest songs, electronic dance music, and music from every corner of the earth. I love how our worship holds space for this plurality of experiences and faiths, rooted in justice and guided by love.

—Camille Hatton

Our Ministry

Rev. Cheryl M. Walker

Every Sunday, before worship services start, John sweeps the walkways in front of the church. Rain or shine, John is there, making sure there is a clear path for people to enter the building. Inside, Agnes is setting up the sanctuary. She checks the microphones, makes sure there are enough candles, and even provides a glass of fresh water for the preacher. Later on, Tess will carefully remove the used candles from the sandbox, knowing that each candle represents something special to the person who lit it. Karla comes early that day; she wants to make sure to get a seat near the windows looking out onto the garden. Her work as a hospice chaplain was especially hard this week, and she needs to be in sacred space with the living, both people and trees.

Jeremy is rehearsing the choir. They're still having difficulties with one passage, and he wants them to sound harmonious and glorious during the service, as they usually do. Meanwhile, Mary is sharing the excitement of last week's march for justice in the state capital. She is pleased that so many people responded to her call and showed up, again. Donna is checking the classrooms to see that there are the right supplies for each class and enough teachers for that day. She stops to speak with David and Gabriella, who have been coteaching the third-grade class this year. Paula arrives with the fresh-baked cookies she makes every week for coffee hour. The youth are delighted by them every time. Bill and Suzy are in the kitchen, making coffee. It's the first week of the month, and they always make coffee the first week of the month.

All of these people are doing ministry. Some of them are paid, but most are not. Some do their ministry inside of the church; some do it beyond its walls. Most of them wouldn't think of what they do as ministry but as something they do for their congregation or organization. The one person not mentioned is the person who holds the title of minister. We know that they do ministry, but we should remember that they are not the only ones doing ministry.

Defining Ministry

What is ministry? Simply, it is what we do consistently in order to serve our congregations, our organizations, and our faith, Unitarian Universalism. What distinguishes a ministry from volunteering is that it is done regularly. John sweeps the walkways every Sunday. Mary coordinates social justice in her congregation every week. There is a consistency that makes it a ministry rather than a single volunteer opportunity.

Ministry is done by laypeople, by religious professionals, and by the clergy. Within Unitarian Universalism, we have a concept of shared ministry. We understand that ministry is not the responsibility of a single person in a congregation or an organization; everyone within the congregation or organization shares it. Everyone is ultimately responsible for the well-being and care of a congregation or Unitarian Universalist organization. There are defined roles and defined levels of authority and power, but ministry has little to do with power and authority; it has to do with service. We share ministry because we share service to our organizations.

Lay Ministries

In our congregations, laypeople perform a myriad of ministries. Some ministries are as simple as being responsible for ensuring there is coffee on Sunday mornings (some people think this is the most important ministry in the congregation). Some are as complicated as serving a term on the board of trustees, creating a vision and policies for the congregation. Lay ministries are essential for any congregation to thrive. In most of our congregations, the day-to-day functioning of the congregation is not the responsibility of the laity; it is the responsibility of the staff. However, when laypeople take on ministries within a congregation, the congregation can realize its mission and vision to a much greater extent than when it relegates ministries to its professional staff.

Our social justice ministries are an example of lay ministry making a difference in whether a congregation merely talks about social justice or is actively engaged in its communities, doing social justice. Our caring ministries help deepen the connections within a congregation when laypeople are actively involved in the care of the membership. We are stronger, and our lights shine brighter, the more our laity shares the ministry of our congregations and our association.

Religious Professionals

Our religious professionals serving within and beyond our congregations each have unique ministries. Whether they are clergy, religious educators, musicians, administrators, or membership coordinators, their ministries are vital to the health and well-being of Unitarian Universalism. Our religious professionals dedicate themselves to their ministries and the professional exercise of those ministries.

If you participate in a Unitarian Universalist congregation or organization, you can be assured that the people in whom you will place your trust are well trained and are held to a high standard of professional conduct. While the qualifications for religious professionals vary by the type of ministry, all religious professionals are of value to people in the congregations and organizations where they serve. Every professional ministry has an association that, among other things, outlines a professional code of conduct to which its members adhere. Unitarian Universalism is dedicated to ensuring that our religious professionals provide people with the best practices of their ministry. And we believe that it is essential to our present and our future that we honor the work of all our professional ministries.

Our Clergy

While we recognize that there is shared ministry within our congregations, it is usually the clergy alone who hold the title of minister, though this is changing. In some cases, other religious professionals hold the title of minister, and the clergy may hold the title of pastor. There are no rules about what clergy persons call themselves. Each congregation has a different culture regarding the naming of its clergy. Some have a very informal relationship and call the clergy by first name. Others use the title reverend or doctor as appropriate. Some, usually in the American South, use the title of pastor. However we may name the clergy, theirs is a particular ministry within our congregations and our faith communities.

The other day, I was speaking to a member of the congregation where I serve; they remarked that they felt they could share their current struggles with me because when I had asked on Sunday how they were, they knew I meant it. They said to me, "Most people ask, but they don't really want to know, but I know that when you ask, you really do want to know. I trust that. I trust you."

At the heart of ministry is trust. You should be able to trust your minister. And your minister must work to earn your trust. No one should immediately expect or be granted trust; it is something that must be earned and re-earned through the years. Our clergy earn trust through their training, through the ritual bonding of a minister and a congregation, through their adherence to the highest standards of our practice, and simply through the one-on-one interactions they have with the people where they serve.

Training in Trust

The journey to ordained ministry begins with a call. Something within the person calls them to follow a path that will lead to ordination. Some people hear it when they are young; some hear it later in life. Ministry is a second career for a large percentage of our ministers. For many women, the idea of becoming a minister was not one they thought they could pursue until they were blessed with Unitarian Universalism. This is true for many of our LGBTQ+ ministers as well. While many other faith communities will not allow women or LGBTQ+ folks to become ministers, Unitarian Universalism does. In all honesty, it was not easy for us to accept people from the margins into our ministry, and we still have our struggles, but we do not have barriers.

Once a person feels the call to ministry, their formal training and assessment begin. They must go to seminary, which is usually three years. They are required to do an internship, usually, but not always, in a congregation. They must do at least one unit of clinical pastoral education, most often by serving as a chaplain in a hospital, where they learn how to be present with people in their most tender of moments. And they must take a battery of psychological exams to be sure they will be capable of performing the duties of ministry. At the end of the road of preparation, there awaits the Ministerial Fellowship Committee, which will assess their fitness for ministry. If all goes well, they will have completed the first part of their training, the first step in earning trust.

Rituals of Trust

The right to ordain is solely the purview of congregations. This is a long tradition from our Unitarian forebears (the Universalists ordained people at their conference meetings). The act of ordination is one of the most important rituals a congregation performs. In the ordination ceremony, a lifelong bond is made between a congregation and a minister that no outside body can break. The congregation, through the act of ordination, says to the world, "We trust this person to be a Unitarian Universalist minister." And the minister makes a commitment to the congregation that they will always live up to the trust placed in them.

For ministers who will serve in congregations, there is another ritual bond of trust called an installation. It is the right of our congregations to choose their own ministers. Through a selection process, aided by the Unitarian Universalist Association, congregations vote to "call" a minister. Unlike faith traditions with hierarchies, Unitarian Universalism gives each congregation the right to say in whom they will place their trust. When they have decided, there is a ritual during which the minister pledges to uphold the trust put in them by the congregation, and the congregation pledges to treat the minister with respect and fairness.

Building Trust

The trust between a minister and the people of the congregations and organizations where they serve is an ongoing process. Although ministers are trained in seminary, their training does not end there. And while rituals formalize the trusting relationship between a minister and congregation, the ritual alone does not build the bond of trust. The minister must earn the trust every day, so they are continually learning and growing, both as a minister and a person. To do that, they need the company and help of other ministers.

Our ministers are expected to be members of the Unitarian Universalist Ministers Association (UUMA), which provides continuing education and collegiality. Additionally, the UUMA has a strong code of professional ethics and conduct to which ministers must adhere. When you trust a minister, you know that they are being held to a high standard of conduct and that the UUMA, along with the Unitarian Universalist Association, will ensure that they perform to those standards.

Ultimately, the interaction between you and your minister is what truly builds a trusting relationship. Your minister will be there for you when you are in need and when you are celebrating the passages of life. Your minister will be there for you to inspire you to a better life and to help shape a better world. Your minister will be there for you; on that, you can place your trust.

We Serve Together

Ministers do ministry, religious professionals do ministry, and laypeople do ministry. We all need each other in different ways. Our Unitarian Universalist ministry encompasses a wide variety of gifts and talents. Our congregations are places where we welcome people of good hearts and open minds to find a place for their own ministries.

Julia's staffing of the welcome table is a ministry that invites newcomers to feel right at home the very first time they come. Katie's ministry of caring means everyone who is in the hospital gets a visit and a teddy bear. Mark and Esther's ministry of music brings depth to the worship experience. Greg's administrative ministry keeps everything running smoothly, making space for the creativity of other ministries. Jesse's service on the board of trustees is a ministry of vision for the future of her congregation. Then there is Rev. Marie, the minister, head cheerleader, comforter in chief, rabble-rouser, inspirational speaker, friend in a time of need, keeper of tissues, giver of hugs, and toiler in the vineyard of souls. All are welcome to find their passion and turn it into service to our congregations, our communities, and our Unitarian Universalist faith. All are welcome to discover their ministry.

I have given my life to Unitarian Universalist ministry. As a young UU child, I was taught to “be like water” and to admire the flowing river. In this world of sharp lines and divisions, I was taught to celebrate the web of all life that really can and does hold us all. Ours is a religion, I quickly learned, that values growth, change, twists, and turns—we flow on, just like the rivers; ours is a traditions of flowers blooming and new life breaking forth into the world. Every day, as a UU minister, I invite people to “be like water,” to open their hearts a little wider, to demand justice, and to embody love. The religious community is the embodiment of the love that held me as a child. And now I carry this love and share it with people every day.

—Rev. Nic Cable

Our Religious Education

Nao Bethea and Jessica York

Chances are you're reading this because you're writing your own story of religious exploration in this moment. Perhaps you want to learn more about Unitarian Universalism, either as a newcomer or as a lifelong UU whose story of faith is still unfolding. You may be on a specific quest for truth and meaning or in search of any safe harbor amidst stormy seas. And although many people find Unitarian Universalism through journeying, this faith is not a destination but a journey itself.

Unitarian Universalists believe that faith is not static. We believe that the search for meaning in our lives does not call for beliefs that are set and already formed but for beliefs that make sense within our own experiences, wisdom of the world, and reason. This is a living faith that develops over time, and each person's experience of it can shift in both depth and breadth. So we speak of faith development as an important aspect of religious life, one that is an active, rather than a passive, endeavor. Learning, growing, and transforming as a UU is both a privilege of our living faith and a responsibility—part of our covenant with each other. UU congregations provide a myriad of ways to engage in faith development. One of the most important of these is through religious education.

As a tool for deepening and widening our faith development, religious education provides dedicated time to distinguish the values that are the foundation of our lives and determine how we can live them more fully. It provides a brave space for you to ask the questions you need to ask, both big and small: *Is there a God? What happens when you die? How do I live a life of integrity? How do I love my neighbor in a world full of fear, anger, and division*? Religious education programs bring people together to support each other in the work of making meaning in their lives. They also inform us about the living tradition that Unitarian Universalists have written so far—the contexts and lessons learned that could be vital for us today.

Both Unitarians and Universalists have honed a philosophy of religious education over the centuries based on active inquiry. Contemporary UU religious educator Joy Berry puts it this way: "Growing faith is more practice and process than prediction or product, more art and story than exact science." The aim of UU religious education is to explore the conditions for liberation—learning, unlearning, and relearning social-emotional skills and community practices which allow us to fully live into our values. We practice engaging our different identities and experiences through curiosity and dialogue, developing greater awareness of our shared humanity and how to sustain communities of safety and belonging.

Lifelong, Multigenerational Learning

Unitarian Universalist faith development is a lifelong journey of learning in matters of the heart and spirit. There is no point of arrival, only different vantage points. We understand that the personal quest for meaning is informed as we age by new experiences and respectful engagement with people who hold different ideas from our own. We are never finished becoming who we can be. We can always be more empathetic; show up more often for justice; care for the sick, the lonely, the brokenhearted; and create more love in the world. We all live our highest values imperfectly, and we can all commit to do better. Our religion does not ask you to be born again. We are instead challenged to bring all that we already are—our identities, life experiences, failures and fears, hopes and dreams—and to go on a journey of transformation. If your religion is not helping you to be a better person, what good is it? There is no original sin here. You will not be asked to confess sins weekly or to wear a hair shirt. Yet this is a place where you can admit your imperfections, knowing that instead of making you less human they actually make you more so. This is a faith that can accompany you through all your life stages: the joys and the sorrows, times of troubling doubt and times of sweet clarity.

In Unitarian Universalist community, we create overlapping circles of people to guide us, to teach our values, help us make decisions, and show us how to make our values real in the world around us. For example, many congregations offer religious education opportunities in groups of similarly aged people and in multigenerational groups.

Multigenerational learning acknowledges that wisdom can come to us from people of any age and is crucial to building the beloved community. Youth share their budding fresh perspectives of the world and their place in it in Coming of Age programs and youth-led services. Middle-aged adults leading preschoolers in meditation enables the sharing of gifts and sends a message that spiritual practices can help anyone at any age stay centered in an overly busy world. Parents and caregivers share how they are trying to guide their children in the ways of compassion. Children learn ways to confront bullies. Elders reflect upon the legacy they wish to leave. Young adults wrestle with and point to parts of our traditions or "old ways" that may no longer serve us. We also believe that a cycle of teaching and learning characterizes the best educational formats, so teachers come ready to learn from participants and participants understand that they are welcome to bring the knowledge they already possess.

Our children and youth are used to education; their brains are wired to absorb incredible amounts of information. As we grow older and take on more responsibilities, we inevitably seek refuge in a more predictable way of interpreting the world around us. We are often reminded by our young people that the world is more wonderful than we experience for ourselves. And sometimes, we're lucky enough to be called to unlearning and transforming our faith by the wisdom of our young UU elders.

Community as Curriculum

Unitarian Universalist religious education programs include stories, teachings, and practices from many sources: direct experience, humanist teachings, the words and deeds of prophetic people, and wisdom from the world's religions, including Judaism, Christianity, and Islam (with which we share historic roots), and earth-centered religions past and present. Our cosmology and theologies are wide: there are no guidelines of statements for what we commonly believe about the supernatural. We each draw from many sources and in learning, sharing, and discerning together, we continue co-creating a living tradition.

Unitarian Universalist religious education is based on the experiences of our communities, where we practice the ideas that are passed down to us and among us, and we practice being willing to be transformed by what we find there. We learn from the community members we worship, study, work, play, grieve, and celebrate with and from the larger Unitarian Universalist movement, including our history. We draw inspiration from the stories of people who have lived into their principles and values, and we learn from the times when we have fallen short of our ideals as individuals and as communities. We also bring into our communities all of the influences that formed us—our ancestors, our cultures, our lived experiences, the people we love, our joys and heartbreaks, and our challenges and blessings. When all of who we are is welcome and when all of our unique selves are together, faith development is nurtured for all of us. Ultimately, what we learn from each direct experience with each other is at least as important as anything we learn in a religious education classroom.

Unitarian Universalists work sincerely to practice radical inclusion. Our religious education programs are full of people with diverse identities: many ethnicities, races, genders, abilities, sexual orientations, and backgrounds. They are a microcosm of the world we need to live and thrive in. We practice our faith most fully when we engage in learning and relationship with those who are different from us, actively engaging with our differences in ways that expand our perspective, deepen our compassion, and possibly even recalibrate our values and ethics. Growing our circles beyond those with the same beliefs, identities, and backgrounds as ourselves can lead us to recognize common human needs and feelings that imbalanced power structures have suppressed out of ignorance, fear, greed, and hatred. Together we can explore how to inspire greater love and vitality, and how to practice repair, grace, and care as we're able when we encounter mistakes, disagreements, or harm. By learning how to navigate difficulties together, we also create antidotes and discernment around the polarizing, maladaptive patterns in our wider communities and world.

Together, we keep exploring the parts of this faith that both feed and challenge us, seeking common strands within and among communities. These strands hold us together and create sites of healing from division and isolation. At its heart, Unitarian Universalist religious education is centered on love: opening to love, being loved, practicing love, questioning love, and growing love.

Justice

Unitarian Universalists believe that working for justice is a faithful activity and that we are all responsible for helping to create a better world. Accordingly, our religious education includes learning about the root causes and history of injustice and turning our learning into action for congregations, local communities, and the wider world. We are a long way from creating the heaven on earth we all desire. In our religious education programs, we explore how to get to that place—within ourselves, our communities, and in the wider world. If there were easy answers, we would be there already. But each day, we can use our lives to go about the work of transforming the world into a place of peace and love. And as Paula Cole Jones, one of our distinguished lay leaders, says, "You cannot transform the world without being transformed yourself." Reflecting on social justice activities afterward together helps us integrate the collective practice of our faith to the context of the rest of our lives and our place in the wider world.

Spiritual Practice and Rituals

Coming into a religious education workshop, you may see preschoolers planting and nurturing a garden, kindergartners moving through a labyrinth in silence, a seventh grader creating a mandala, a high school youth journaling, or a young adult reading a prayer they wrote in a poetry slam. We know that our spirits are nourished in many different ways. Our religious education programs allow all ages to sample different practices and encourage participants to include spiritual practice in their daily lives.

We also use rituals to mark the transitions and transformations in our lives. Workshops include everyday rituals, like lighting a chalice, singing UU hymns, or building an altar. Religious education programs celebrate new life with child dedications, offer coming of age and bridging workshops to mark young people's journey in faith, and may offer sage-ing retreats to recognize the changing nature of our faith, which lasts even into elderhood.

It is comforting to know that we are not alone in the faith journey of deepening and widening our spirits. We join in the community of the faithful to have our values affirmed and challenged. We come to build relationships and learn stories that are different from our own. We lift each other up, finding strength in community. May the many paths of religious exploration lead you to a place where your spirit finds peace, joy, and love.

Unitarian Universalism taught me courage. It taught me to take risks for what is right, to not be afraid to speak up for my values, even if it means being a lone voice. It helped me learn to organize for justice; to love abundantly and boldly; and to trust in the saving power of joy and laughter, of community and song. I am grateful to have been raised from my earliest days to honor the core values of respect and compassion for all. I have been regularly encouraged to wrestle with questions of truth and meaning. And I have received affirmation of my own agency and my ability, indeed, the ability of everyone, to make a positive difference.

—Rev. Susan Frederick-Gray

Our Work for Social Justice

Rev. Elizabeth Nguyen

The Unitarian Universalist feminist and peace activist Margaret Moseley called social justice work moving mountains one stone at a time. Margaret was born in Boston in 1910. She dreamed of being a nurse, but being African American, she was turned away from all of the nursing schools in the city. She went on to help found Cooperative Way and Freedom House and to lead the anti-McCarthyism movement and the Community Church of Boston.

We move mountains, one stone at a time; as Unitarian Universalists, our journey is to transform the big and the small, to transform ourselves, and to transform the world. Universalism means no one is outside of the circle of love and no one is disposable. We stubbornly seek out the spark of the divine in each other, no matter what. Interdependence means none of us is truly tree until we are all free, and our thriving is bound up in the earth's thriving. We struggle for liberation from the violence of white supremacy, sexism, ableism, classism, and heterosexism. Our covenants mean we make promises to our communities to honor love and justice above all else.

Unitarian Universalism is there in the youth group at the Pride Parade, covered in rainbows and glitter. Unitarian Universalism is there in the climate activist on trial for doing what she sees as necessary to return to a right relationship with the earth. Unitarian Universalism is there in the congregation providing space, childcare, and dinner for the coalition organizing after the police killing of a young person. Unitarian Universalism is there in the justice team that accompanies an undocumented person to her court dates, raises money for her legal fees, and builds community with her family.

Unitarian Universalism is for those who have seen the arc bend toward justice and for those who doubt it will ever bend but know we must organize as if our lives depend on it anyway, because they do. Some theologies say that only some people are saved. From those theologies flows a world where people are criminalized for their identities—for being Muslim, transgender, Black, undocumented. Our theology says that we are all saved, and that salvation is what we strive to build now, for each other. So we resist any laws, policies, or practices that deny anyone their humanity. We know that now on earth is our chance to create heaven. We know that love crosses borders and prison walls, lives in queer families and disability justice organizers, thrives among trans young people and working-class elders.

Some religions think of suffering as something that happens to individuals, which individuals must heal from. As Unitarian Universalists, we know suffering is also collective. And that we heal collectively. The original wounds of slavery and genocide in this country cannot be fully repaired in any one individual life. Instead, we work for collective healing and liberation.

Our Unitarian Universalist justice ancestors like Margaret Moseley remind us that we are not alone and that we come from a long legacy of healing and repair. Our legacy includes those who have sacrificed for justice and those who have been cowardly in the face of injustice. We know that behind the struggles for the abolition of slavery, for voting rights, for LGBTQ justice that can look so pretty in the newspapers, there is messiness, betrayal, falling short, and the seduction of choosing comfort over convictions.

Unitarian Universalism is there, too, reckoning with all the ways we have broken our vows and all of our imperfection. With the parent trying to figure out how to get through the day and show up for that community meeting. With those of us who are white, trying to speak up and act out against white supremacy and also love ourselves and our families. With those of us who are people of color, trying to unapologetically live our values, knowing the cost that can come to our careers and our spirits. We are already saved from perfection. And Unitarian Universalist community, songs, prayers, and spiritual practices are there to remind us when we forget.

For me, it's singing. Because when I'm singing, I'm breathing. When I'm terrified that the meeting is going to fall apart, when someone I trust and look up to is giving me feedback that's hard to hear, or when I'm about to knock on someone's door or engage in direct action or sit down with the elected official or write the grant, that's when I try to remember that I can sing.

Don't get me wrong: I'm not a good singer. But it's not about being a good singer. It's about remembering that singing brings me back to courage, possibility, and enough space for spirit.

Practicing Under Pressure

Unitarian Universalism is a community of people practicing together. We practice living our values, not just on

Sunday mornings or on holy days. We practice embodying our deepest truths under pressure, when our backs are against the wall. This is a thorny spiritual truth—that who we are on our worst days is who we actually are.

Organizer Caitlin Breedlove often says that we respond to crisis with our highest level of training, not with our highest values. Buddhist teacher Rev. angel Kyodo williams writes that "today's progressive leaders must systematically and lovingly prepare us to tolerate the inherent discomfort of change now in order to wedge open the way to transformation in the future. They must do this under pressure; they must do this while in motion; and they must do this with and on behalf of others."

Pressure reveals to me where I am so practiced. And where I have never done this before. Or to say it another way, pressure reveals to me where I embody my values—they are not separate from me—and where they are the first things I forget about. Some people say we have to do a new thing twenty-one times for it to become a new pattern of behavior, three hundred times for it to become instinct, three thousand times for personal transformation, and ten thousand times for mastery.

Whatever we practice, we get really great at. If we practice flexibility, humility, courage, we get strong at those things. If we practice rigidness, ego, cowardice, we get strong at those things. If we practice saying no one ever trained me to do that or we don't have enough or I'm afraid to try, that muscle gets more and more practiced.

When my father's family came to the United States as refugees from Vietnam, a woman named Ruth in Wisconsin opened her home and welcomed them. Ruth had somehow gotten enough practice living her values under pressure that she was willing to have her family's life transformed by mine. There is a thing that happens for so many of us: that some things are news and other things are family. For some of us, increased Islamophobia is news. For some of us, increased Immigrations and Customs Enforcement or surveillance of activists or stop-and-frisk or addiction or climate chaos or cash bail are issues or headlines. For some of us, it's family.

As Unitarian Universalists, we live our values because they are morally right but also because we know that we are family. And we are going to fight for each other like family because, in the end, if we believe in our words about interdependence, they actually are.

So we practice together. So that it is not our first or second time trying to live our values under pressure. We will practice at least the three thousand times needed to embody our values in our communities.

The Hard Way

I once saw a little sign, carved in wood, that read, "There is only the hard way." Many of us have been harmed by theology that told us that suffering was a sacrifice that would bring us closer to God. Many of us were told that our suffering would redeem us. Even when we knew that actual redemption would have been to be set free from the suffering to begin with. And many of us are only here because of the sacrifices of others. So much of what is possible to carve out in this world requires some giving up, some letting go, some sacrifice.

That is the truth of that little wooden sign: there is no easy way. There is only the hard way. In particular, the work of justice often asks us to do impossible, hard, terrifying things. Folks with more privilege sometimes get caught up here. "If it's hard, maybe we are doing it wrong," we tell ourselves. We are lulled by our experiences of choosing between a hard choice and an easier one. Folks with less privilege know that many of our choices are between a horrific choice and a horrific choice. And we learn to live with that and keep going.

Many of us want to do the right thing, the just thing, the generous thing, and also not have to give anything at all. We want to share our opinions but not actually donate our evenings, our weekends, our doing-the-dishes-while-on-the-conference-call to get to understand the work enough to be able to offer meaningful thoughts. We want people to trust us and let us shape the vision but not actually risk inviting folks out to tea, dinner, beers, or church to build a relationship that endures and carries us forward. We may want to post the cute meme without actually making the phone call to the city councilor or state representative. We want to be part of that powerful, courageous, game-changing, direct action without the long-past-midnight planning meetings, the messy decision making, the frayed relationships, and the constant wondering if this is even worth it. We want to talk about being bound together in interdependence but do not actually want to give our guest room to a stranger, give a paycheck to someone we've never met, or turn our schedule inside out to do what needs to be done.

The word *sacrifice* might be too much mess for some of us, too tainted by oppression and coercion. What matters more is that we are willing to live our lives in the shape of what is being asked, not hope that what we are asked to do will fit the shape of our lives. When we believe that the work of justice should fit our lives, instead of being willing to let our lives move to fit it, we cede so much of our power.

I can't unknow the sacrifices that my parents, my grandparents, and my ancestors made for me. I can wish they weren't necessary or that there had been another way, but that's an alternate world. In this one, what others have done for me becomes fuel for figuring out how to "keep moving with your heart hurt and your body starting to tire," as Toshi Reagon sings. One of the principles of Movimiento Cosecha is sacrifice: "Our seeds come from the tree of sacrifice. We honor the hard work of all the people who bring the gifts to the movement. We believe people's work in Cosecha is for the collective well-being of everyone and not for personal gain or to advance individual interests." Mary Hooks, in her work leading Southerners on New Ground, offers this mandate: "to avenge the suffering of our ancestors, to earn the respect of future generations, and to be transformed in the service of the work."

As Unitarian Universalists, we lean into the hard questions. What do we value that we are willing to let go for something we value even more? What must we do to earn the respect of those who come after? What is the hard way we are willing to go?

Humility

What about when we disagree? It happens all of the time. You have probably read some things here that you have disagreed with. We know that our religious ancestors disagreed. Communities fractured over the abolition of slavery and integration, just as others were strong and united in their convictions. Our spiritual communities are full of big and little disagreements—from what to put on our banners to what role religious people and communities should play in the work of justice.

Our spiritual muscles are what allow us to stay in community across difference, differentiate the fake disagreements from the real ones, and sort out when to be humble about what we might not understand and when to be unwavering in what we know to be true. In the journey of justice, just like the journey of the spirit, we know that new truths are always being revealed. And we know that spiritual truths persist that we must never compromise. Harm to any being is harm to the web of all life. While there are absolutely wrong behaviors, there are no wrong people. The circle of love holds us all.

As Rev. Rosemary Bray McNatt has written, "The truth is this: If there is no justice, there will be no peace . . . if we cannot bring justice to the small circle of our individual lives, we cannot hope to bring justice to the world. And if we do not bring justice to the world, none of us is safe and none of us will survive. Nothing that Unitarian Universalists need to do is more important than making justice real—here, where we are."

In a world where we are not yet all free, it is a precious thing to reorient ourselves, over and over again, toward love, justice, and liberation. This is the hope, the work, and the promise of Unitarian Universalism. To ground us in possibility and connection. To energize us as we build neural pathways, change hearts, uplift spirits, and honor all our bodies. To remind each of us that our freedom is bound up in others' freedom and that their freedom is bound up in ours. I am grateful every day for a faith and a movement that has the potential to bring all our journeys of spirit and connection together to usher in a better world. And I'm really excited that I get to be in it with you.

—Rev. Mykal Slack

Our Communities

Rev. Nancy McDonald Ladd

There is a story of an old-time evangelist who paid a visit to the home of a prospective new member of his congregation. The two men sat down before a fire in a cozy living room and struck up some gracious conversation. The conversation wound its way through many topics until this new churchgoer started to talk himself out of it all, arguing that it was possible, perhaps even preferable, to be a believer without participating in the life of a community.

You can probably imagine the conversation. It is nothing particularly new. It might have gone something like a conversation you have had yourself. There are just so many other things to do with one's time, and, by extension, one's life, without ever gathering together with other people to do overtly spiritual or religious things. You may know deep in your own bones that it's possible to find the holy under a canopy of trees. You may, in fact, be capable of finding your spiritual center all by yourself, in the company of your own journal or a scrap of always imperfect knitting.

Nothing about our Unitarian Universalist tradition would dispute or contradict those experiences. We affirm that the sacred can be found in the middle of the everyday and is not confined to the spaces of traditional sanctuaries and congregational worship. We do not have a corner on the market for holiness or a sense that a spiritual life can only be lived in certain ways or only on a Sunday morning. Many of us need quiet spaces to allow for meaning and purpose to show up in our lives, especially when the pain and struggle of a hurting world feel so very loud.

And yet, our story doesn't end there. To come back for a moment to where we started—the preacher and the possible future congregant sitting before a roaring fire—you'll remember the familiar claim that a person doesn't really need to be in a community to do the things that nurture a spiritual life and extend out to help heal the world.

In that fireside conversation, I imagine that perfectly reasonable argument for isolation over community hung in the air for a moment between those two. Perhaps there was silence. At which point, the wizened old preacher leaned forward a bit in his chair, took up the iron poker on the hearth, and pulled a single bright flaming coal out of that fire before him. He knocked that bit of captured flame onto an isolated square of stone on the cold floor, and the two watched silently as the coal slowly dimmed and went out.

When glowing red had turned to ash, the preacher turned his head and looked silently at the person before him. “Sir,” the future congregant said, “I believe you have made your point.”

By our nature, human beings are social creatures. We make meaning through our connections to one another and the experiences we have that point toward a sense of purpose and strength so much larger than our isolated selves. In this way, Unitarian Universalists are not unique. We, too, have a glowing coal—of purpose, meaning, and hope—that is kept alight in part because we choose to remain connected to the enkindling presence of others. We, too, experience the loneliness and alienation of these days, even as we find ourselves connected in new and exciting ways through communities both within and beyond our congregations. Like others, we reach out for connection and community as a way to keep that burning coal alight.

Most teachers, preachers, and community organizers worth paying attention to go out of their way to remind all of us that we need to take care of both our bodies and our spirits. We cannot heal the world if we do not first attend to our own well-being. As such, self-care is an essential practice of the spiritual life, especially in the presence of the great injustice and polarizing political pressures of our time. And yet, as the writer and poet Cole Arthur Riley has said, "Self-care alone won't save us. Community is a necessary risk."

Of course, community is not any easier than isolation. It's complex. People are messy. A shared story takes longer to write than one you might author all on your own. And yet, that risk of reaching out and connecting across differences and divisions is an essential part of the Unitarian Universalist spiritual life.

In our tradition, these essential pockets of community often form around a central location, such as a church or a building, although not always. A congregation is a group of people who gather together to form a community within our tradition, and you can find Unitarian Universalist congregations meeting in venerable sanctuaries that are hundreds of years old and around tables in coffee shops and family homes. Some of our communities gather on campuses and in online spaces, reaching out to one another in ways that would have been unimaginable just generations ago. The tradition of forming a community within Unitarian Universalism is both very old and ever-evolving.

We're not a members-only club, although we certainly foster a sense of belonging to and with one another. We're not a school that runs through a prescribed curriculum, although everything that happens in the community is a form of learning. We're certainly not a political organization, although our deeply held values often have political consequences.

Our communities do not merely recreate what can be found in the secular, commercial, or political world. Instead, we are a broad and diverse religious community that approaches questions through the lenses of pluralism and care.

For us, a commitment to pluralism means that no single story or experience is put at the center of the people's meaning making. Unitarian Universalists come from many religious backgrounds and no religious background at all. Because we hold many different identities, our communities celebrate what it means to be intentionally multiracial and multicultural. Our resources and shared practices are designed to lift up a multiplicity of perspectives so that dominant stories and experiences don't crowd out the diverse voices of the whole.

As an intentionally pluralistic tradition, our communities draw strength from the various beliefs, stories, and viewpoints that our members and participants bring with them, modeling a community-forming power that is centered more on the people's willingness to change and to be changed by one another than on the specific beliefs or positions of any one individual among us.

By adhering to our historical affirmation of pluralistic values, we also commit ourselves to practices of community care. We aspire to build communities where we all hold responsibility for each other's well-being. When that glowing coal of meaning and purpose seems to dim, we move closer to our community so that it might be rekindled. When one among us is particularly at risk, we try to use the power and privilege of the whole to make us all safer together.

Given this ethic of community care, Unitarian Universalists were among the first faith traditions to move toward large-scale precautions during the Covid-19 pandemic. We took our sanctuaries and sacred spaces and imagined them in new ways that allowed us all to be safer. The community uprooted itself in service to the larger ethic of care. Even as we came back together in our physical spaces, we did so with the deep intention of holding those most at risk in a network of care.

Responding to the historical and contemporary harms of racism, oppression, and marginalization in our congregations and in our wider culture, Unitarian Universalists' years-long collective work toward systemic change has invited us to widen the circle of our care and concern far beyond historically privileged identities. That work continually reminds us of the power of compassion, acknowledging the etymology of the word *compassion—com*, meaning "with" or "together," and *-passion*, derived from *pati*, which means "endure, undergo, experience."

Together, we are asking, "Can we feel what another experiences?" If we can approach even a glimmer of true compassion, we must always ask how we can make tangible choices in our collective and individual lives that reflect the ethic of communal care.

Our communities are places of deep nurturance for the spiritual journey. They are pluralistic models for what it takes to foster belonging without falling back into the age-old habits of othering or excluding. They are platforms in which to practice a deep form of communal care that could, in turn, influence society and the world around us.

Throughout history, we know that the great thoughts and the great thinkers, the great acts and the great doers, the great resistance movements and the great resistors did their work as part of a collective creation. This experience of community is not easy to come by in this radically interconnected yet deeply atomized world. In this way, community is itself a collective creation that has the power to affect others far beyond the circle of people gathered together.

An intimate, honest, and imperfect community may, in fact, be the most powerful tool imaginable for transformation of ourselves and amplification of our deeply held values. And so, our communities are places of nondoctrinal but deeply faithful nurturance of those values. They are places of connection that keep our own flame of hope burning long enough that we can, in turn, offer some illumination to a hurting world.

Our faith begins with acceptance. All of us are part of a spirit of life and love that we do not need to earn. We insist that our differences are sources of our strength and beauty. Come as you are.

—Rev. Dr. Bill Sinkford

A Living Tradition to Meet the Moment

Rev. Ashley Horan

If you have found yourself in the sanctuary of a Unitarian Universalist congregation over the past thirty years, chances are, you've picked up *Singing the Living Tradition*, known by many as the "gray hymnal." The title comes from a contemporary phrase that refers to a quintessential characteristic of Unitarian Universalism (and our Universalist and Unitarian lineages before us). This is our foundational belief that although we are the inheritors of the spiritual, theological, and ecclesiological wisdom of our religious forebears, "revelation is not sealed"—that is, our understandings of the divine, human morality, justice, and religious community will inevitably continue to evolve in response to the world around us. We believe the work of both personal and communal religion is to draw upon the spiritual gifts passed down to us by our ancestors while continually interpreting and embodying them through the lens of our own contemporary context. In contrast to religious traditions that hold central the inerrancy of scripture, the absolutism of dogma, or the infallibility of religious authorities, Unitarian Universalists believe that faith and religious practice must continually change and adapt over time. Ours, we are clear, is a *living tradition.*

Perhaps the most famous articulation of this defining characteristic of our faith comes from Theodore Parker, a nineteenth-century abolitionist, Transcendentalist, and Unitarian minister. In 1841, Parker preached an ordination sermon entitled "A Discourse on the Transient and Permanent in Christianity," in which he argued,

> There seem to have been, ever since the time of [our religion's] earthly founder, two elements, the one transient, the other permanent. The one is the thought, the folly, the uncertain wisdom, the theological notions, the impiety of man; the other, the eternal truth of God.

Parker believed that the *purpose of religion* is to help humans live out certain transcendent, unchanging values that honor and express the will of God—namely, "the divine life of the soul, love to God, and love to man." But the *structures of religion*—the doctrines we espouse, the ways we worship, the organizations we build, and the practices we engage in—are by their very nature products of their time, culture, and context and are therefore prone to corruption, co-optation, and irrelevance precisely because they are created by humans, not God. Knowing this, Parker urges us to devote ourselves to the purest essence of faith while holding the forms lightly, ensuring we neither allow them to divide us (petty sectarian disputes) nor mistake them for our most unwavering commitments (idolatry).

Unitarian Universalist history contains myriad examples of our religious ancestors identifying something in our theology, ecclesiology, or polity that no longer served its intended purpose and either adapting or abandoning it to be more relevant and impactful for the current times. Today's Unitarian Universalism, for example, is still deeply influenced by the system of congregational polity laid out in the Cambridge Platform of 1648—but thankfully, we no longer get our funding from taxes as the established religion of the state, require that ministers be reordained when they leave a particular congregation, or expect "repentance from sin and faith in Jesus Christ" as the prerequisite for church membership. More recently, in 2024, following a multiyear study process required by our bylaws, the delegates of the Unitarian Universalist Association's General

Assembly voted to adopt entirely new language to articulate our foundational values, replacing the long-standing Principles—yet another evolution of the transient to better express the heart of the permanent for our times.

But not all such reckonings with our living tradition arise from planned processes and discernment; sometimes they are forced upon us because of tectonic shifts in the culture and context in which we live. The landscape in which I write in early 2025, during the first one hundred days of a second Trump administration that is actively eviscerating the administrative state and attempting a fascist coup on behalf of white Christian nationalism, is fundamentally different from the one that Unitarian Universalists navigated fifty, ten, or even five years ago—both within our faith and in the broader society. The current moment is rife with both existential challenges and liberatory opportunities that demand we ask ourselves, yet again: which aspects of our faith are so essential that without them, we would no longer be Unitarian Universalists?

As non-creedal people, we have myriad articulations of our shared faith. My own distillation of what is permanent in Unitarian Universalism would include the understanding that we are, each and all of us, born into, worthy of, and inseparable from a love so encompassing that we can never stray outside its reach. That there is no one singular truth, and the exquisite multiplicity of human perspective and experience is our greatest blessing and most valuable resource. That we are profoundly responsible for and connected to one another and to the earth. That the only hells with which we need concern ourselves are here, in this life, of our own creation. And that no one is disposable; therefore, the work of our lives is to create the conditions of possibility for all people to live lives of freedom, dignity, and prosperity.

These are our timeless values and commitments. But the forms we design to give them life in practice (governance models, liturgical practices, mission statements, program offerings) are rightly transient. Because climate chaos, shifting demographics, evolving politics, and inequitable financial realities—and the spiritual needs these dynamics create—define the current moment, we must be ready to nurture what is already flourishing, retire or reimagine what has outlasted its usefulness, and explore new possibilities to expand the impact and relevance of our faith for these times.

How will Unitarian Universalism meet this moment? Perhaps we will learn from congregations that have provided sanctuary to asylum seekers and weave an expanded network of radical material solidarity to transgender and nonbinary people, climate refugees, and those crossing state lines for abortion care. Maybe we will learn that deep small-group ministry programs, embodied spiritual practices, weeknight gatherings for song and ritual, and multigenerational meals are more effective for faith formation in our context than the traditional format of Sunday-morning worship. Or we might decide that our endowments and buildings should be leveraged for missional purposes beyond the survival of our own congregations and thus invest our assets into building innovative hubs of resistance and resilience that prophetically serve our neighbors and communities.

The stakes are too high for us to lose touch with who Unitarian Universalists fundamentally are or to cower from growing into who we are called to become. Being stewards of a living tradition means remaining unshakably grounded in the permanent while holding the transient with gentle curiosity. The world, in all its beauty and brokenness, is inviting us to meet this moment with all of the clarity and courage we can muster. Will we accept the invitation?

We often refer to Unitarian Universalism as a living tradition. What makes a tradition a living one? I would argue that it is a testament to our being unabashedly in and of the world—yes, even the hard and yucky bits that meet us, especially those aspects that lead us to change and be changed. We understand this: only that which is alive may change, and only that which can change may remain alive. Nature preaches this gospel across eons, written in DNA, fossil records, and every creature's dreaming of a new day. Transformation flames to life in our wheel of values, yet it is not a wild or unmeasured change we speak of but one rooted in love and tradition. So, it is true that tension may arise, but this is the stuff of life, the dissonance that resolves in song, the energy that spirals us into a new day, a new life, a new love.

—Rev. Juniper Meadows

Our Roots

Dr. Dan McKanan

Unitarian Universalists possess a rich tradition and many different ways of relating to it. Some argue that because we lack a shared doctrine, it is our common history that holds us together. Others relish the freedom to draw on multiple spiritual sources without being bound to any. Some take pride in knowing that unitarian and universalist ideas about a single, all-loving God are as old as Christianity itself, and our shared values have still more ancient roots. Others stress the distinctly American flavor of our movement, noting that the Unitarian and Universalist denominations (capital Us) were born in the wake of the American Revolution. Still others tell the stories of our partner churches in Transylvania, the British Isles, the Khasi Hills of India, and the Philippines, insisting that their histories are our legacy as well.

Ancient Roots

Given this diversity, one might begin telling the Unitarian Universalist story at many different points in time. UU Buddhists and UU Pagans claim a heritage that is older than Christianity. But most Unitarian Universalists trace their roots to the biblical traditions of Judaism and Christianity. The ideas of "unitarianism," that God is one being, and "universalism," that God's love will save all humanity, can be found in the scriptures of ancient Judaism. For millennia, Jews have declared daily that "the Lord is one" and cherished the hope that "all the families of the earth shall be blessed."

These beliefs were part of the rich diversity of early Christianity. Searching the scriptures, some theologians found hope that all humans and even the devil would be restored to harmony with the divine. The official church refused to teach that this was certainly so. Yet Catholic and Eastern Orthodox theologians continue to teach it as a possibility. The idea of unitarianism was more controversial. As the Roman Empire was becoming Christian, church leaders declared that Jesus Christ, the Holy Spirit, and God the Father were a Trinity, sharing a single divine substance. Those who found this unbiblical or too paradoxical created a rival church—with its own hierarchy and dogmas. Even after that church died out, unitarian beliefs were despised as heresy by most Christians.

Unitarianism experienced renewal at the time of the Protestant Reformation in the sixteenth century. Protestants cherished the principle of sola scriptura. They relied entirely on the text of the Bible. Those who took this principle furthest rejected the idea of a state church, insisting that Christians should choose voluntarily to follow Christ's path. Among their modern descendants are the Amish and Mennonites. One small wing of this movement also rejected the idea of a Trinity as unbiblical. They planted churches first in Poland and then in the multireligious borderland of Transylvania. Mindful of Jewish and Muslim neighbors, Transylvania's Unitarian king embraced a policy of religious freedom.

The Polish church eventually disappeared, but Unitarianism survives in Transylvania. Unitarian ideas reappeared in seventeenth- and eighteenth-century England and Ireland. Those who held them, including the philosopher John Locke, blended a commitment to biblical authority with the Enlightenment's stress on reason. Unlike the deists on one side and orthodox Christians on the other, they refused to choose between reason and revelation. Their first congregation was the Essex Street Chapel. Organized in 1774 by a former Anglican priest named Theophilus Lindsey, it set the tone for similar congregations in the American colonies. Early British Unitarians included the entrepreneur Josiah Wedgwood, women's rights advocate Mary Wollstonecraft, and Jamaican-born radical Robert Wedderburn, the first Black Unitarian minister. Universalist ideas appeared in England during the seventeenth century, when they were first championed by Gerrard Winstanley, founder of the socially radical Diggers. Later in the century, Jane Leade and the Philadelphia Society linked universal salvation to mystical visions of paradise restored. A century later, revivalist James Relly taught Universalism on the grounds that Christ had died to save not individuals but all humanity as a single body.

Founding of the United States

Although European movements influenced their North American counterparts, the origin of Universalism and Unitarianism in the United States did not involve the transplanting of European institutions to new soil. Nor was there a single "founding moment" for either tradition. Several different groups held unitarian or universalist beliefs. They came together only gradually.

The first people in North America to teach universal salvation may have been Germans who came to

Pennsylvania for religious freedom. Their mystical Christianity also inspired them to live in celibate communities, practice alchemy, and wait for the end of the world. The first explicitly Universalist congregation was planted in Gloucester, Massachusetts, by John Murray, an English immigrant who had learned from James Relly that an all-powerful God had predestined everyone to be saved. But the largest number of early Universalists came out of Baptist churches in western New England. Skeptical of educated ministers, they read the Bible for themselves and cherished debates with neighbors who read it differently. These diverse communities began to organize a General Convention in 1790. They had little in common other than fervent belief in God's love and fierce opposition to state-sponsored religion. This put them in conflict with the Puritan or "Standing Order" congregations of New England, which received tax support well into the nineteenth century.

The first Unitarian congregations in the United States were inspired by Englishman Joseph Priestley. Priestley was a chemist who discovered oxygen, a friend of Thomas Jefferson, and a theologian who insisted that Jesus was no more than human. In 1784, his writings convinced the minister of King's Chapel in Boston to eliminate references to the Trinity from that congregation's liturgy. Ten years later, Priestley immigrated to the United States and helped found congregations in Philadelphia and rural Pennsylvania.

Like the Universalists, Priestley was wary of state-sponsored religion. But ironically, several Standing Order churches in the neighborhood of Boston embraced a milder form of Unitarianism. They believed that Jesus was more than human but less than divine. They also stressed that humans are good enough to mirror God's love. Whereas their Puritan ancestors had seen humans as depraved, they had absorbed the optimistic Enlightenment philosophy taught at Harvard College. The debate over these new ideas caused a schism among the churches in Massachusetts. Although the Unitarians were reluctant to separate from their more orthodox siblings, they created the American Unitarian Association in 1825.

Both Universalists and Unitarians vested significant power in local congregations. Long after the Unitarians abandoned Puritan theology, they continued to honor the Puritans' Cambridge Platform of 1648, which affirmed that "there is no greater church than a congregation which may ordinarily meet in one place." Each congregation was bound together by the free covenant of its members, and each had the authority to choose its own minister and other leaders. Universalist practice was more varied than

Unitarian, but it was often even more fiercely decentralized. In some places, congregational polity allowed the wealthiest laypeople to monopolize power. But at their best, self-governing congregations served as seedbeds of democracy in the larger society.

Each fledgling denomination had a theological champion. The Universalists' Hosea Ballou was a fiery debater who delighted in clever interpretations of the Bible. He taught that Jesus had died not to appease an angry God but to soften the hard hearts of humanity. And he took the radical position that even the worst sinners will go straight to heaven. Other Universalists speculated that some would be purified by temporary hellfire.

The Unitarians' William Ellery Channing was a reluctant radical. He loved peace and helped organize opposition to the War of 1812. He hesitated to organize a separate denomination but eventually became its most eloquent spokesman. He also hesitated to speak out against slavery, a practice that had enriched many members of his family. Channing's growing sympathy for abolition eventually alienated him from the wealthy congregation he had served for decades.

Although Channing was a Unitarian and Ballou a Universalist, each man appreciated aspects of the other tradition. Ballou was a proud champion of Priestleyan unitarianism. Channing did not affirm universal salvation, but his faith in the human capacity to grow in likeness to the divine drew on the same spiritual streams as ancient universalist ideas. While God's love was the heart of Ballou's theology, Channing stressed the benevolence that humans could hold in common with the divine. Because of class differences, the two men scarcely acknowledged one another, although they ministered in the same Boston neighborhood. Today's Arlington Street Church is heir to both of their congregations.

Ministers were not the only people who helped build up the two traditions. John Murray's wife, Judith Sargent Murray, was a powerful leader and advocate of women's rights. She began demanding equal access to education in 1779 and composed the first Universalist catechism three years later. Lucy Barnes wrote letters to spread the Universalist faith. Catharine Sedgwick, one of the nation's most popular writers, incorporated Unitarian themes into her novels. Unitarian Hannah Adams expressed her liberal religious convictions in one of the first dictionaries of world religions. And while many Universalists championed labor unions, Boston Unitarians Francis Cabot Lowell and Nathan Appleton brought the industrial revolution to the United States and built great cultural institutions on its profits.

Heretics, Reformers, and Institution Builders

Three different sorts of leaders helped nineteenth-century Unitarianism and Universalism evolve. First, there were the heretics—unfettered thinkers who reached beyond inherited theologies. Abner Kneeland, who called himself a pantheist rather than a Christian, left the Universalist ministry to lead Boston's Society of Free Enquirers. He was the last person jailed for blasphemy in the United States. Ralph Waldo Emerson shocked the faculty of Harvard Divinity School by urging future ministers to preach from their own souls rather than from scripture. The Transcendentalist movement he launched transformed American literature as well as the Unitarian ministry. During the 1850s, roughly half of all Universalist ministers embraced the Spiritualist movement, which sought a scientifically verifiable path to religious truth. A generation later, Unitarians and Universalists were the first to embrace Darwinian science as an ally rather than an enemy of faith.

Other Unitarians and Universalists were reformers. The heart of their religion was building a society founded on love. Universalist shoemaker William Heighton helped launch the labor movement by calling for a political party composed entirely of "working men." The brothers Charles and John Murray Spear, both Universalist ministers, befriended prisoners and fought to end the death penalty. Unitarian Lydia Maria Child risked her career as a writer of children's books by demanding the immediate abolition of slavery. Ministers Theodore Parker and Thomas Wentworth Higginson were so opposed to slavery that they took up arms to defend fugitives from the South. Adin Ballou, who served both Unitarian and Universalist congregations, was a staunch abolitionist, absolute pacifist, and creator of a utopian community. His writings on nonviolence inspired Leo Tolstoy and Mohandas Gandhi. Unitarian Peter Clark of Cincinnati was the first Black American to run for Congress as a Socialist. Universalist and Unitarian women were among the first to be ordained in the United States. Antoinette Brown Blackwell, Lydia Jenkins, and Olympia Brown combined ministry with agitation for women's suffrage.

Contemporary UUs cherish the memory of the heretics and the reformers. But we would not remember them at all if it weren't for the institution builders. Among the Unitarians, denominational president Henry Whitney Bellows led the way in making space for both Transcendentalists and liberal Christians in a single church. And the Universalists' "grasshopper missionary," Quillen Shinn, hopped to many unlikely corners of America with the message of God's limitless love.

Reaching Out

Unitarians and Universalists never held a monopoly on liberal religion. Many Unitarian Universalists today hold views similar to the eighteenth-century deists and nineteenth-century Freethinkers. Those groups taught a "religion of reason" that only gradually found a home in our tradition. Some of the founders of Unitarianism and Universalism were active Freemasons, and from that tradition, they took a commitment to religious tolerance and brotherly love. Unitarians and Universalists have long felt a kinship with the Quaker tradition, with its emphasis on the "inner light" in each person. They also reached out to the Reform movement in Judaism, which stressed ethics over ritual. The Ethical Culture movement founded by a rabbi's son, Felix Adler, abandoned belief in God altogether and worked closely with the radical wing of Unitarianism.

By the turn of the twentieth century, many Congregationalists, Methodists, and other Protestants were preaching a liberal theology similar to that of the Unitarian and Universalist founders. They also proclaimed a "social gospel": True religion was about building a better world. Unitarians and Universalists worked closely with them. At Harvard, Francis Greenwood Peabody introduced sociology into the curriculum for future ministers. More radical activists created organizations that we now think of as secular. Universalist Charles Vail was the national organizer of the Socialist Party. Unitarian Roger Baldwin was the first leader of the American Civil Liberties Union. Unitarians Mary White Ovington and John Haynes Holmes were among the founders of the National Association for the Advancement of Colored People. With Universalist Clarence Skinner, Holmes also launched a network of activist "community churches." Among them was Egbert Ethelred Brown's Harlem Community Church, an important meeting place of dialogue between Black Americans and West Indians, and between activists with socialist and with Black nationalist ideals.

Reformers like Holmes, Brown, and Skinner worked closely with a new wave of heretics. Calling themselves "humanists," these heretics put their faith in science and humanity rather than God. Humanist leaders John Dietrich and Curtis Reese both came to Unitarianism from more conservative denominations. Several Unitarians and one Universalist, Clinton Lee Scott, signed the "Humanist Manifesto" that announced their ideas to the world. Meanwhile, other Universalists redefined their tradition to focus on the wisdom of all world faiths.

Once again, institution builders were flexible enough to win the heretics back. As leader of the Massachusetts

Universalists, Scott invited a Unitarian humanist named Kenneth Patton to launch an experimental congregation. Its members studied global faiths and contemporary science, treating their church as a workshop for the future. Unitarian president Frederick May Eliot embraced humanists and reached out to Universalists, hoping both groups would help him build a united liberal church.

Unitarianism finally transcended its New England roots through the fellowship movement of the 1940s, 1950s, and 1960s. In communities from Montgomery, Alabama, to Boulder, Colorado, laypeople created congregations without ministerial oversight. Many were closely tied to colleges or research centers. Others provided a church home for radical activists in conservative neighborhoods. Some of the fellowships have grown into thousand-member churches. Others remain small and feisty.

Toward Beloved Community

The new congregations brought their energy into the Unitarian Universalist Association, founded in 1961 after more than a century of parallel evolution and cooperative projects at both the local and national levels. A few congregations and individuals still proudly call themselves "Unitarian" or "Universalist." Most others, especially those who have come to the tradition since consolidation, claim a fully "Unitarian Universalist" identity. Unitarian Universalists played a vital role in the social change movements of the 1960s. Building on the legacy of the NAACP founders, Unitarian minister Homer Jack helped launch the northern sit-in movement in the 1940s, and he guided our tradition's social justice work in the 1960s. Most of the White lawyers who supported Martin Luther King Jr.'s work in Montgomery were members of the local UU fellowship. UU minister James Reeb and UU housewife Viola Liuzzo were martyred in Selma, Alabama, where they had joined hundreds of UU ministers in response to the murder of a local Black American activist named Jimmie Lee Jackson. Reeb had been a community minister at Boston's Arlington Street Church. Two years later, that same congregation hosted an interfaith liturgy at which opponents of the Vietnam War prayed together as they burned their draft cards.

Not everyone agreed on the best way to foster justice and peace. Many Unitarian Universalists, both Black and White, embraced the Black Power movement of the late 1960s. They hoped that economic and cultural empowerment would make beloved community possible. Others feared that Black Power was a betrayal of the integrationist ideal. The General Assembly of 1968 committed $1 million to economic development projects led by Black individuals. Debate over that decision consumed the denomination for the next two years. Leaders reduced funding for empowerment, citing a budget crisis. People on both sides left the tradition, hurt and angry. Others stayed or returned, making the struggle against racism and for beloved community one of our defining commitments. Recent expressions of this struggle include many congregations' embrace of an "Eighth Principle" condemning White supremacy; the work of Diverse and Revolutionary Unitarian Universalist Multicultural Ministries (DRUUM) and Black Lives of UU (BLUU); and the activist push, begun in 2017 and embraced by presidents Susan Frederick-Gray and Sofía Betancourt, to ensure that our national leadership reflects the beloved community we strive to become.

Unitarian Universalism has also transformed itself through its encounter with feminism and LGBTQ+ liberation. When Rev. James Stoll came out as gay in 1969—the first minister in any tradition to do so—he was embraced by other Unitarian Universalists. Our pioneering sexuality education curriculum, About Your Sexuality, was expanded to honor sexual diversity. Similarly, a small contingent of women ministers swelled to a majority within a few decades. The 1977 Women and Religion resolution began a process of removing sexist language and practices from our shared life. As women explored goddess-centered practices, they made neo-paganism an integral part of the spiritual mosaic of our faith. Unitarian Universalist congregations and individuals were at the forefront of the struggle for marriage equality at the turn of the twenty-first century. And since 2004, Transgender Religious professional UUs Together (TRUUsT) has led the way in making the ministries of transgender Unitarian Universalists both visible and valued.

If the late 1960s could be considered the tumultuous adolescence of Unitarian Universalism, our movement has since settled into a stable maturity. Membership declined rapidly in the 1970s but has been relatively steady since then. This is because of our appeal to spiritual seekers, social activists, and interfaith families. It is also because our movement, once heavily concentrated in the Northeast, has become much more evenly spread across the United States. Another indication of maturity was the process, completed in 2024, of revising the "Principles and Purposes" section of our bylaws. While many religions prize doctrinal stability, our bylaws mandate a thorough reconsideration of our core identity every fifteen years. The commission created for this purpose received a mandate to "articulate core UU theological values," with a particular emphasis on the value of love, so cherished by Hosea Ballou, William Ellery Channing, and other founders. After two years of movement-wide dialogue, the 2024 General Assembly approved, by an 80 percent majority, an articulation of the values of interdependence, pluralism, justice, transformation, generosity, and equity, with love quite literally at the center. It also clarified that mutual accountability, inclusivity, and freedom of belief are all essential tools for free congregations.

In UU congregations today, Christians, humanists, Jews, Buddhists, Muslims, pagans, seekers, and others build religious community together. We join in the fight for justice, and we help one another find sustaining spiritual practices. Our diverse national leadership guides us on the journey toward beloved community—stumbling frequently, but always striving to learn from the stumbles. As we continue moving forward, we look back with gratitude to the heretics, reformers, and institution builders who came before us.

For centuries, our way of religion has drawn the circle of faith larger—theologically, spiritually, and organizationally. This has often meant living with pushback from narrow-minded, orthodox religious and cultural leaders and communities whose beliefs and leadership make them reluctant or incapable of meeting the expectations of an increasingly diverse population. We are grateful for the possibilities and promises that come with the richness and challenge of diversity and inclusion.

—Rev. Dr. Fredric Muir

Beloved

Rev. Victoria Safford

In a gathering of ministers convened I-don't-remember-when and I'm-not-certain-where, our convenor, warm and smiling, lit the chalice and invited us forward, one by one, for a ritual. We'd been asked to write a microscopic sermon, one or two short sentences, and share it in the circle as a blessing for our colleagues and for our Association, which was then (as now, as ever, as always, and by definition) in a time of change and Deep Discernment regarding whence we come, and how, and whither:

> For our opening chapel service, please come prepared to share with your colleagues in just a few words: What is it you hope the people will receive on Sunday morning in your congregation's service, whether they are visitors or lifelong members, elders or young children? What, for you,

is the essence of our faith? What gospel are you preaching?

This convening was about that. The ritual would anchor our discussions. Quiet music began.

One by one, my colleagues spoke, movingly, courageously, some in Sunday voices, thoughtful and well reasoned, some haltingly and tearfully, all generous, all kind. No bluster here, no rhetorical flourishes or arrogant edges, but only grace, amazingly, their words anointing us, the crumpled cards and scribbled slips of paper in their hands placed like offerings upon the altar. There was no pulpit here to hide behind; there were no robes or stoles to shroud us. One by one, these ministers, old and young, people I'd known and admired for so long and many I didn't know, shared blessings from a vulnerability deep inside themselves with integrity that was at once heartbreaking and heartening. They *testified.* The softening silence after each one was like a kind of sacrament. Then and there, decades past my ordination, I was converted to Unitarian Universalism all over again. One by one, my colleagues spoke of love.

I've never been an extemporaneous preacher. I really don't know how or why I spoke the words I did when my turn came. Somehow, I heard myself telling them, and meaning it, urgently:

You are beloved of God.

(Who was it who said that preachers preach unfailingly the sermon that they themselves most need to hear?)

You are beloved of God.
It is so easy to forget this.
Our calling on this earth is to remember and remind each other,
with every move we make,
every action,
every breath.
Our calling is to remember and remind each other
without ceasing
who we are, and what,
which is beloved.

Something like that. I scribbled it in pen on the palm of my hand and soon sweated it away.

Here, with the compelling power and the solace, the blessed assurance, of my comrades' benedictions in my head, I realized that for me, this is the heart of it, this implicit, inherent "beloved-ness." Behind the silky scrim of woven words each week lay this hope, this intention, this aching aspiration, that whether they "believed in God" or not, and whether or not I did, the people would know themselves beloved, which is to say, worthy, with a place, as the poet says, "in the family of things," a place no more and no less exalted than anyone's place, or the place of the grasses, the trees, the birds of the air, and the fish of the sea, a holy, wholly undisputed, rightful place on this, our common ground. To know themselves, to know ourselves, beloved without question, is the place where we begin. And from there, by our actions, by our choices, by our art, by our risks, by our work and tears and prayers and mutual support, by our solidarity and singing (lullabies to children and chanting in the streets), by our tenderness, and when it is required, rage—by our love, in other words—to remind each other. This is our calling in this world.

I care—a great deal—about the precision of language, and theological speech in particular. I know the lethal and life-giving potency of words and the ease with which sloppily chosen words may be weaponized or just misunderstood, and yet . . . I don't want precision or theology or semantics to get in the way of this conviction, this hunch, this simple, somewhat radical (to the very root) claim about love. As music and dancing, paintings, poems, and prayers insist, metaphor speaks sometimes with more fluency, more light, more prophetic possibility and more pastoral tenderness, than the deadening thud of literal, prosaic explanations. I've not been a minister long enough, I've not been a person long enough, to know much about God at all. But I believe we are called to move through our days as if we are beloved of God, as if we all belong, we ourselves and everyone else, and every living thing. When I say, "You are beloved of God," I mean *you are beloved, OF COURSE*. You just are.

Now and here, in this unlikely, perhaps unreplicated, gorgeous world, this shimmering, sorrowing world, we exist, together. No scientist, no sorcerer, no sacred text can ever fully tell us why or how it's happened, this existence—whether we ask our whole lives long in the idiom of astrophysics or a child's bedazzled wonder. We are here now, and we all belong. Beloved. And therefore, my work, however imperfect at the end of each day, my work and my joy is to strive to act accordingly, as if in your presence (whoever you are, wherever on this earth you are), I were in the presence of the holy. I have no other words to describe it, this love that guides us, calls us, heals us, and holds us in its hands.

Resources

UU World, the magazine of the Unitarian Universalist Association (UUA), aims to help its readers build their faith and act on it more effectively in their personal lives, their congregations, their communities, and the world. The print magazine is published quarterly in February, May, August, and November. You can subscribe or read a weekly issue of the free online edition at uuworld.org.

The UUA also publishes a number of pamphlets intended to answer questions you may have about Unitarian Universalism. You can read these online by visiting uua.org/pamphlets.

Side with Love, the Organizing Strategy Team of the Unitarian Universalist Association, serves as the hub for the denomination's justice and organizing work. This work harnesses the power of love to confront systems of oppression and build a world where people can thrive. Rooted in UU values, Side with Love equips individuals and communities through political education, leadership development, and spiritually grounded action—working in deep partnership with frontline movements for liberation. Learn more at sidewithlove.org.

The following books are available from inSpirit: The UUA Book and Gift Shop at uua.org/bookstore:

Takiyah Nur Amin and Mykal Slack, eds. *BLUU Notes: An Anthology of Love, Justice, and Liberation.*

Sofía Betancourt, ed. *Love at the Center: Unitarian Universalist Theologies.*

John A. Buehrens. *The Universalists and Unitarians in America: A People's History.*

Patricia Frevert, ed. *Welcome: A Unitarian Universalist Primer.*

Keith Kron and Susan A. Gore, eds. *Coming Out in Faith: Voices of LGBTQ Unitarian Universalists.*

Paul Rasor. *Faith without Certainty: Liberal Theology in the 21st Century.*

Meg Riley, ed. *Testimony: The Transformative Power of Unitarian Universalism.*

Voices in Unitarian Universalism Series

Wayne Arnason and Sam Trumbore, eds. *Buddhist Voices in Unitarian Universalism.*

Kendyl L. R. Gibbons and William R. Murry, eds. *Humanist Voices in Unitarian Universalism.*

Leah Ongiri and Marti Keller, eds. *Jewish Voices in Unitarian Universalism.*

Jerrie Kishpaugh Hildebrand and Shirley Ann Ranck, eds. *Pagan and Earth-Centered Voices in Unitarian Universalism.*

Kathleen Rolenz, ed. *Christian Voices in Unitarian Universalism.*

Songs and Readings

Lifting Our Voices: Readings in the Living Tradition

Singing the Journey

Singing the Living Tradition

For Children

Pam Baxter. *A Cup of Light.*

Jennifer Dant. *Unitarian Universalism Is a Really Long Name.*